HOMEMADE JAMS
JELLIES AND PRESERVES

(FRUIT BUTTERS, CONSERVES
AND MARMALADES)

THE ENTHUSIAST

The Enthusiast exists to celebrate and promote genuine enthusiasm for enriching, elevating and entertaining subjects, including, but not limited to, art, history, literature, philosophy, science, cooking and sport.

What's Your Passion?

 http://enthusiast.cc

 TheEnthusiast@Enthusiast.cc

 @EnthusiastThe

 http://pinterest.com/enthusiastthe/

 http://www.facebook.com/EnthusiastThe

Copyright, 2013, by
The Enthusiast
All rights reserved - no part of this book may be reproduced in any form without permission in writing from the publisher.

ISBN / EAN

EBook Edition   1595837418 / 9781595837417
Standard Edition   1595837426 / 9781595837424

CONTENTS

- Introduction & General Tips pages 4-7
- Jams pages 8-15
- Jellies pages 16-23
- Preserves pages 24-29
- Conserves pages 30-35
- Fruit Butters pages 36-41
- Marmalades pages 42-47

General Instructions - Read Me!

The fun foods in canning, and often the ones which produce the most satisfaction for the home canner, are the butters, conserves jams, marmalades and preserves. Although many have tried, few have succeeded in imitating the distinctive flavor of choice homemade products. The smart home canner knows, or can easily learn, how to combine orchard-fresh fruits with sugar, add spices or extracts to please the taste of her own family and cook the mixture in small batches.

With butters, conserves, jams, marmalades and preserves, you can use your imagination. The natural fruit flavor can be changed or emphasized by adding a tiny pinch of salt, a small amount of spice, extract, orange peel, lemon juice, to any of the recipes.

Tests for the Jellying Point:
1. Sheet test

Jelly drops first are light and sirupy

Then they become heavier and show signs of sheeting.

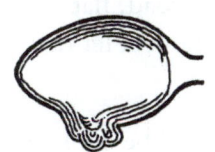

When jelly point is reached, jelly breaks from spoon in a sheet or flake.

Dip a cool metal spoon into the boiling jelly mixture. When two drops form together and sheet off the spoon, the jelly should be done.

CANNING

2. Temperature Test

Before cooking jelly, take the temperature of boiling water with a jelly or candy thermometer It is necessary to find out at what temperature water boils in your locality because the boiling point differs at different altitudes and under different atmospheric conditions Cook the jelly mixture to a temperature of 8°F higher than the boiling point of water in your locality At that point the concentration of sugar will be such that the mixture should form a satisfactory gel.

Tips

1. Prepare fruit by washing it gently in cold running water, or washing it in several changes of cold water, lifting the fruit out of the water Sort. Remove hulls (caps), cores, pits, seeds or skins; leave whole, slice or chop as stated in the recipe, discard all spoiled potions.

2. Weigh or measure fruit after preparing. When possible, weigh, for results will be more perfect. The general rule of 3/4 pound sugar to 1 pound prepared fruit is used when making conserves, jams and marmalades. Preserves usually require pound for pound fruit and sugar. Kitchen scales are a profitable investment if "jam-making" is a favorite pastime in your household.

3. Up to 1/3 of the granulated sugar may be replaced with corn syrup. Up to 1/2 of the granulated sugar may be replaced with honey Honey changes the fruit flavor and may even mask it.

4. A large, heavy kettle of 8-10 quart capacity with a broad, flat bottom is an essential in "jam-making." This size kettle will let the fruit and sugar mixture bubble and cook rapidly.

5. Conserves, jams, preserves and marmalades should all be cooked in small batches. Do not double recipes. Sugar should be stirred over low heat until it dissolves. When the sugar has dissolved, the mixture should be cooked rapidly (boiled) for a bright and sparkling finished

product. To prevent sticking and scorching, the fruit mixture should be stirred frequently as it thickens.

6. All butters, conserves, jams, marmalades and preserves thicken more as they cool. Thickness is hard to judge when the product is hot. The jellying point test is an excellent one to use see page 5-6.
For a softer product, shorten the cooking time for a firmer product, lengthen it.

7. Times given in the recipes are approximate and a guide only. Conditions vary when making jams so it is impossible to state exact times. For instance, the size and weight of the kettle used, the humidity of the day and the altitude all enter into how long it takes to thicken or reach the jellying point.

8. Process butters, conserves, jams and preserves 10 to 20 minutes at simmering (180-185F°) In a water bath canner. Read each recipe for processing times.

9. Prepare fruits check jars for nicks, cracks and sharp edges on sealing surfaces. Wash jars in hot soapy water. Rinse leave in hot water. Prepare lids and bands according to product instructions.

10. Remove fruit mixture from heat. Jar leaving ¼ inch head space. Seal all fruit products airtight. Process as recommended.

11. Store in dark, dry, reasonably cool area.

A Note on Pectin

Many home canners prefer to use commercial pectin when making jams and jellies pectin should be used according to the manufacturer's instructions, they should easily adapt to the recipes in this book. Or make your own pectin: Two pounds apple pulp (or skins and cores), 4 cups water, juice 1 lemon, boil for 40 minutes. Press the juice through a cloth, then strain this juice through cloth without pressure. Boil juice rapidly 15 minutes. Seal in sterilized jars and use for jelly making. Add 1 cup apple pectin for each cup of other fruit juice used.

JAMS

Jams are soft jellies with the fruit left in. They may be made of berries or large fruits. The fruit should not retain its shape in the finished jam so it is cut or crushed before or during cooking. Jams are made without water when possible for the same reason as jellies, long cooking impairs both flavor and color. The resulting consistency should be thick, smooth, clear and not quite so firm as marmalade though the distinction is difficult to maintain. Because they are quick and easy to make, because they have so many uses, jams are one of the most popular ways to preserve fruits.

Briefly, jam making consists of crushing the fruit, adding proportionate amounts of sugar, heating until the juice is thick and clear and pouring into a sterile container. The juices of many jams will "sheet" (see page 5) when they are done.

As in jellies, fruits low in pectin are helped by the addition of apple or currant.

Jams must be closely watched and stirred while cooking. Pack while hot in sterile jar- and seal at once.

When measurements are given by weight, the fruit being easily weighed before cooking. If you have no scale cook to pulp and measure. Where a pound of fruit is called for in the recipe, substitute 2 cups pulp; where a pound of sugar is called for, substitute 2 cups sugar.

CANNING

Freezer Berry Cherry Jam

4 cups prepared fruit
(1 pint fully ripe blackberries or 1 ½ pints red raspberries and 1 pint ripe sour cherries)
5 ¼ cups sugar
¼ cup water
Pectin as per product instructions

Crush berries, pit and grind sour cherries. Combine in bowl with sugar, let stand 10 minutes. Mix pectin and water and bring to a boil, boil 1 minute stirring constantly (per product instructions.) Stir into fruits, continue stirring about 3 minutes. Pour into jars, leaving ¼ inch head space. Affix caps. Let stand until set (30 minutes to 24 hours) Freeze until desired, will keep in refrigerator for a week. Makes 5 cups.

Fig Jam

2 quarts chopped fresh figs
(about 5 pounds)
¾ cup water
6 cups sugar
¼ cup lemon juice

To prepare chopped figs, pour boiling water over figs; let stand 10 minutes. Drain stem and chop figs. Measure and add and add ¾ cup water and sugar to figs. Slowly bring to boiling, stirring occasionally until sugar dissolves. Cook rapidly until thick. Stir frequently to prevent sticking. Add lemon juice and cook 1 minute longer. Pour, boiling hot, into hot jars. Adjust caps. Process 10-15 minutes in boiling water bath at simmering temperature (180-185°) . Yield: about 5 pints.

JAMS

Peach-Raspberry Jam

4 cups prepared fruit
(about 2 lbs. ripe peaches and 1 pint red raspberries)
6 cups sugar
¼ cup lemon juice
Pectin as per product instructions

Peel, pit and crush peaches, add crushed berries to make 4 cups. Combine fruit and lemon juice in a very large saucepan. Stir sugar into fruit. Place over high heat, bring to a full rolling boil, boil hard one minute. stirring constantly. Remove form heat and stir in pectin (per product instructions.) Skim off foam. Pour hot into hot jars, leaving ¼ inch head space. Affix caps. Process pints and quarts about 10 minutes in boiling water bath at simmering temperature (180-185°) Yields: about 8 cups.

Strawberry Jam

2 quarts crushed strawberries
6 cups sugar

Combine Berries and sugar. Cook until soft, adding only enough water to prevent sticking. Press through a sieve or food mill. Measure pulp. Add remaining ingredients; cook until thick, about 15 minutes. As mixture thickens, stir frequently to prevent sticking. Pour hot into hot jars, leaving 1/4 inch head space. Affix caps. Process pints and quarts about 10 minutes in boiling water bath at simmering temperature (180-185°) Yields: about 2 pints.

CANNING

Freezer Fruit Cup Jam

¾ cup (1 pint) fully ripe strawberries
¾ cup pineapple
(¼ fully ripe medium pineapple)
½ cup (½ lb.) fully ripe pears
½ cup (2 medium) oranges
4 ½ cups (2 lb.) sugar
¾ cup water
Pectin as per product instructions

Thoroughly crush strawberries. Peel, core, and grind pineapple. Peel and section oranges, discard membrane and seeds, crush thoroughly. Peel, core and grind pears; Mix sugar into fruits; let stand 10 minutes. Mix water and pectin in a small pan (per product instructions.) Bring to a boil and boil 1 minute, stirring constantly. Stir into fruits. Continue stirring for 3 minutes. Ladle quickly into containers; cover at once with tight lids. Let stand until set (this may take up to 24 hours); then store in freezer. Makes about 5 ¼ cups.

Blueberry Currant Jam

1 quart stemmed blueberries
2 cups stemmed currants
2 cups water
3 cups sugar

Combine blueberries and 1 cup water; cook slowly 5 minutes. Combine currants add 1 cup water; cook slowly 10 minutes; press through a sieve or food mill to remove seeds. Combine blueberries and currant pulp; cook rapidly 5 minutes Add sugar, stirring occasionally until sugar dissolves. Cook rapidly until thick, about 20 minutes. As mixture thickens, stir frequently to prevent sticking, Pour, boiling hot, into hot jars. Adjust caps. Process 10-15 minutes, in boiling water bath at simmering temperature (180-185°) Yield: about 2 pints.

Paradise Pear Jam

4 cups prepared fruit (1 orange, 1 lemon, 2 lb. fully ripe pears, ¼ cup chopped Maraschino cherries, ½ cup finely chopped citron, and one 8 ½ oz. can crushed pineapple)
5 cups sugar
Pectin as per product instructions

Remove rinds from orange and lemon in quarters; discard about half the white part. Slice rinds, chop orange and lemon, discard seeds. Peel, core, and grind pears. Combine all the fruits, including cherries, citron, and pineapple. Measure into a large saucepan. Measure sugar set aside. Stir Pectin into fruit (per product instructions.) Place over high heat; stir until mixture to a hard boil. At once stir in sugar. Bring to a full rolling boil and boil 1 minute, stirring constantly. Stir and skim. Pour hot, into hot jars. Adjust caps. Process 10-15 minutes, in boiling water bath at simmering temperature (180-185°) Yield: about 7 cups.

Peach Jam

2 quarts crushed peeled peaches
½ cup water
6 cups sugar

Combine peaches and water; cook gently 10 minutes. Add sugar; slowly bring to boiling, stirring occasionally until sugar dissolves. Cook rapidly until thick, about 15 minutes, stirring frequently to prevent sticking. Pour, boiling hot, into hot jars. Adjust caps. Process 10-15 minutes in boiling water bath at simmering temperature (180-185°) Yield: about 4 pints.

For Spiced Peach Jam add 1 teaspoon whole cloves. ½ teaspoon whole allspice and 1 stick cinnamon, tied in a cheesecloth bag to jam during cooking. Remove spice bag before pouring into jars.

CANNING

Nectarine Jam

4 cups prepared ripe nectarines (about 3 lb.)
¼ cup lemon juice (2 lemons)
7 cups (3 lb.) sugar
Pectin as per product instructions

Peel and pit nectarines. Chop fine or grind. Measure into very large saucepan; add lemon juice. Add sugar to fruit and mix well. Place over high heat, bring to a full rolling boil, and boil hard 1 minute, stirring constantly. Remove from heat and at once stir in pectin (per product instructions.) Skim off foam. Stir and skim for 5 minutes to cool slightly and prevent floating fruit. Pour into hot jars. Adjust caps. Process 10-15 minutes, in boiling water bath at simmering temperature (180-185°) Makes about 12 medium glasses.

Gingered Peach Jam

¼ cup finely slivered candied ginger
4 ½ cups prepared fruit
(about 3 ¼ lb. ripe peaches)
6 cups (2 lb. 10 oz.) sugar
Pectin as per product instructions

Measure the ginger into a large saucepan. Peel and pit peaches. Chop very fine or grind. Add to the saucepan. Measure sugar, set aside. Add pectin to fruit and mix well (per product instructions.) Place over high heat, stir until mixture comes to a hard boil. Stir in sugar. Bring to a full rolling boil, boil hard 1 minute, stirring constantly. Remove from heat and skim off foam with metal spoon. Then stir and skim for 5 minutes to cool slightly and prevent floating fruit. Pour, into hot jars. Adjust caps. Process 10-15 minutes, in boiling water bath at simmering temperature (180-185°) Makes about 10 medium glasses.

Apricot Jam

2 quarts crushed peeled apricots
6 cups sugar
¼ cup lemon juice

Combine all ingredients; slowly bring to boiling, stirring occasionally until sugar dissolves. Cook rapidly until thick, about 25 minutes. As mixture thickens, stir frequently to prevent sticking. Pour, boiling hot, into hot jars. Adjust caps. Process 10-15 minutes, in boiling water bath at simmering temperature (180-185°)
Yield: about 5 pints.

Plum Jam

2 quarts chopped tart plums (about 4 pounds)
6 cups sugar
1 ½ cups water
¼ cup lemon juice

Combine all ingredients; bring slowly to boiling, stirring occasionally until sugar dissolves. Cook rapidly almost to jellying point, about 20 minutes. As mixture thickens, stir frequently to prevent sticking Pour, boiling hot, into hot jars. Adjust caps. Process 10-15 minutes, in boiling water bath at simmering temperature (180-185°) Makes about 12 medium glasses.

JELLIES

Jelly is made by cooking fruit juice with sugar. The product should be firm enough to hold its shape when turned from the jar, yet soft enough to be spread with a knife. Whether jellies are clear or translucent depends upon the fruit used and the manner of extracting the juice.

Jelly Tips:

1. Proper amounts of fruit, pectin, acid, and sugar are needed to make a jellied fruit product.

2. Fruit gives jelly its characteristic flavor and furnishes at least part of the pectin and acid required for successful jelly. In order to make a good jelly, a fruit juice must contain the right kind and quantity of acid and the right amount of pectin. Acid is the substance which makes the juice tart or sour. To make a good jelly, the juice should be about as tart as that of sour apples. For best results in making jelly without commercial pectin, use a fruit firm, and just ripe.

3. Pectin is the substance which causes the fruit juice to "jell" and without pectin, no fruit jelly is possible. Some kinds of fruit such as tart apples and Concord grapes, have enough natural pectin to make jelly. Others, for example strawberries, require added pectin. These pectins may be used with any fruit.

4. Acid is needed for flavor and for the gel formation. The acid content varies in different fruits With fruits that are low in acid, lemon juice or citric acid is commonly added If acid seems lacking, usually 1 tablespoon of strained lemon juice added to each standard measuring cup of fruit juice will supply the needed acid.

5. Sugar helps in gel formation, contributes to flavor, and serves as a preserving agent.

6. Suggested Equipment for Making Jelly. Large kettle is one of the essentials We suggest an 8 to 10 quart kettle with a broad, flat bottom This size kettle permits the jelly mixture to come to a full rolling boil without boiling over.

7. Jelly bag which may be made of several thicknesses of closely woven cheesecloth. A jelly bag is needed for straining the pressed juice.

CANNING

Currant - Strawberry Jelly

4 ½ cups juice (about 1 ½ qt. each ripe red currants and strawberries and ½ cup water)
6 cups sugar
Pectin as per product instructions

Stem and crush red currants. Add the water bring to a boil simmer, covered, 10 minutes. Crush strawberries. Place fruits in jelly cloth or bag; Squeeze out juice. Measure 4 ½ cups into a very large saucepan. Measure sugar and set aside. Add Pectin to juice and mix well (per product instructions.) Place over high heat and stir until mixture comes to a hard boil. At once stir in sugar. Bring to a full rolling boil and boil 1 minute, stirring constantly. Stir and skim. Pour hot, into hot jars. Adjust caps. Process 5 -10 minutes , in boiling water bath at simmering temperature (180-185°) Yield: about 6 1/2 cups.

Four Fruit Jelly

4 cups prepared juice (about ¾ qt. each ripe sour cherries, red currants, red raspberries, and strawberries and ½ cup water)
6 cups (2 lb. 10 oz.) sugar
Pectin as per product instructions

Stem, pit, and crush cherries and currants. Add water; bring to a boil, simmer, covered, 8 minutes. Crush raspberries and strawberries. Add to fruits; simmer 2 minutes. Place in jelly cloth; squeeze out juice. Measure into large saucepan. Mix pectin into juice (per product instructions.) Place over high heat; stir until mixture comes to hard boil. Stir in sugar. Bring to full rolling boil, boil hard 1 minute, stirring constantly. Remove from heat, skim off foam. Pour hot, into hot jars. Adjust caps. Process 5 -10 minutes , in boiling water bath at simmering temperature (180-185°) Makes about 10 medium glasses.

JELLIES

Apple Jelly

4 cups apple juice (3 pounds apples and 3 cups water)
2 tablespoons strained lemon juice.
3 cups sugar

Select ¼ firm-ripe and ¾ fully ripe tart apples. Sort, wash, remove stem and blossom end do not pare or core. Cut into small pieces. Add water cover and bring to boil on high heat. Reduce heat and simmer for 20 to 25 minutes, or until apples are soft. Extract juice. To make jelly. Measure apple juice into a kettle. Add lemon juice and sugar and stir well. Boil over high heat to 8°F. above the boiling point of water, or until jelly mixture sheets from a spoon. Remove from heat; skim off foam quickly. Pour jelly immediately into sterilized hot containers and seal. Process 5 -10 minutes , in boiling water bath at simmering temperature (180-185°) Makes 3 to 4 eight-ounce glasses.

Mint Jelly

Pour 1 cup boiling water over
1 cup firmly packed mint leaves

Let stand for 1 hour.
Press the juice from the leaves.
To each cup of apple juice, add 2 tablespoons of the mint extract and bring to a boil. Follow Apple Jelly recipe above.
Just before pouring into jars or jelly glasses, tint the jelly with a few drops of green food coloring. Makes 3 to 4 eight-ounce glasses.

CANNING

Gooseberry - Raspberry Jelly

5 cups prepared juice (about 1 ½ qt. each fully ripe gooseberries and red raspberries and ½ cup water)
7 cups (3 lb.) sugar
Pectin as per product instructions

Crush thoroughly or grind gooseberries Add water, bring to a boil, and simmer, covered, 10 minutes. Crush red raspberries. Combine fruits in jelly cloth or bag; squeeze out juice. Measure into large saucepan. Mix pectin into juice (per product instructions.) Bring to a hard boil over high heat, stirring constantly. At once stir in sugar. Bring to a full rolling boil and boil hard 1 minute, stirring constantly. Remove from heat, skim off foam with metal spoon, and pour quickly into glasses. Process 5 -10 minutes , in boiling water bath at simmering temperature (180-185°) Makes about 8 cups.

Blackberry Jelly

4 cups blackberry juice (takes about 2 ½ quart boxes blackberries and ¾ cup water)
3 cups sugar

Select about one-fourth firm-ripe and three fourths fully ripe berries Sort and wash; remove any stems or caps Crush the berries, add water, cover, and bring to a boil on high heat Reduce heat and simmer for 5 minutes. Extract juice. To make jelly. Measure juice into a kettle. Add sugar and stir well Boil over high heat to 8° above the boiling point of water, or until jelly mixture sheets from a spoon. Remove from heat; skim off foam quickly Pour jelly immediately into sterilized hot containers and seal. Process 5 -10 minutes , in boiling water bath at simmering temperature (180-185°) Makes 3 to 4 eight ounce glasses.

JELLIES

Raspberry - Strawberry Jelly

4 cups prepared juice
(about 1 ½ qt. each ripe red raspberries
and strawberries)
7 ½ cups (3 ¼ lb..) sugar
Pectin as per product instructions

Crush thoroughly red raspberries and strawberries. Place in jelly cloth and squeeze out juice. Measure juice into a very large saucepan. Add sugar to juice; mix well. Place over high heat; bring to a boil, stirring constantly. Stir in pectin (per product instructions.) Then bring to a full rolling boil and boil hard 1 minute, stirring constantly. Remove from heat, skim off foam with a metal spoon, and pour quickly into glasses. Process 5 -10 minutes , in boiling water bath at simmering temperature (180-185°) Makes about 11 medium glasses.

Cherry Jelly

3 cups cherry juice (takes about 3 pounds or
2 quart boxes sour cherries and ½ cup water)
7 cups sugar
Pectin as per product instructions

Sort cherries, wash, and remove stems; do not pit. Crush the cherries, add water, cover, and bring to boil on high heat. Reduce heat and simmer 10 minutes. Extract juice. To make jelly. Measure juice into a kettle. Stir in the sugar. Place on high heat and, stirring constantly, bring quickly to a full rolling boil. Add the pectin and heat again to a full rolling boil (or per product instructions.) Boil hard for 1 minute. Remove from heat; skim off foam. Pour jelly immediately into hot containers and seal. Process 5 -10 minutes , in boiling water bath at simmering temperature (180-185°) Makes 7 to 8 eight-ounce glasses.

CANNING

Orange Jelly

2 ½ cups juice (about 6 oranges)
6 cups (2 ½ lbs.) sugar
Pectin as per product instructions

Add orange juice to grated orange rinds and let stand 10 minutes. Press juice through cloth. Measure juice and sugar into large saucepan, stir, and bring to a boil. At once add pectin (per product instructions,) stirring constantly, and bring again to a full rolling boil and boil ½ minute. Remove from fire, let stand 1 minute, skim, pour quickly. Process 5 -10 minutes , in boiling water bath at simmering temperature (180-185°) Makes about 8 eight-ounce glasses. about 12 medium glasses.

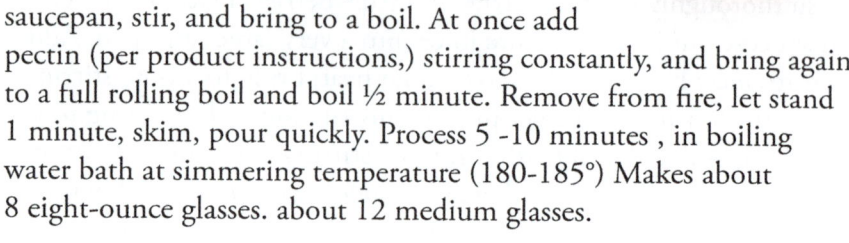

Ripe Plum Jelly

4 cups juice (about 4 pounds fruit)
7 ½ cups (3 ¼ lbs.) sugar
Pectin as per product instructions

Use only fully ripened fruit. Do not peel or pit. Crush thoroughly and add 1 cup water. Stir until mixture boils, and simmer, covered, 10 minutes. Drip through jelly bag. Measure juice and sugar into large saucepan, stir, and bring to a boil. At once add pectin, stirring constantly (per product instructions,) and bring again to a full rolling boil and boil minute. Remove from fire, let stand 1 minute, skim, pour quickly. Process 5 -10 minutes , in boiling water bath at simmering temperature (180-185°) Makes 10 to 11 eight-ounce glasses about 12 medium glasses.

JELLIES

Lime Jelly

1 cup lime juice (about 6 limes)
2 ½ cups water
5 cups (2 ¼ lb..) sugar
Pectin as per product instructions
Green food coloring

Squeeze and strain the juice from limes. Measure 1 cup into a large pan. Add water; mix well. Measure sugar and set aside. Add pectin to juice; mix well (per product instructions.) Bring to a hard boil on high heat, stirring constantly, add food coloring to shade desired. At once stir in sugar. Bring to a full rolling boil and boil hard 1 minute, stirring constantly. Remove from heat, skim off foam with metal spoon, and pour into glasses. Process 5 -10 minutes , in boiling water bath at simmering temperature (180-185°) Makes about 5 ¼ cups.

Grape Jelly

4 cups grape juice (takes about 3 ½ pounds
Concord grapes and ½ cup water)
3 cups sugar

Select about one-fourth firm-ripe and three-fourths fully ripe grapes. Sort, wash, and remove grapes from stems. Crush grapes, add water cover, and bring to boil on high heat. Reduce heat and simmer for 10 minutes. To prevent formation of crystals in the jelly, let juice stand in a cool place overnight, then strain through two thicknesses of damp cheesecloth to remove crystals. Measure juice into a kettle. Add sugar and stir well. Boil over high heat to 8° F. above the boiling point of water, or until jelly mixture sheets from a spoon. Remove from heat; skim off foam. Pour jelly into sterilized hot containers and seal. Process 5 -10 minutes, in boiling water bath at simmering temperature (180-185°) Makes 3 to 4 eight-ounce glasses.

PRESERVES

Preserves are fruits cooked whole or in large pieces in a sugar syrup of such strength that the water is gradually removed from the pulp of the fruit and replaced by syrup. They are then stored in the thickened syrup in which they were cooked.

Since the shape of the finished product is important, the fruit selected should not he over-ripe. The cooking should be rapid, as is the case with any other fruit and sugar product, to prevent loss of flavor and color. However, care must be taken that they shall not cook to pieces. Syrup should always be sufficient to cover the fruit. Its consistency depends on the fruit for which it will be used.

For good results, the substitution of syrup for water in the fruit pulp must not take place too rapidly. Too heavy a syrup will draw the juices from the fruit at once, leaving them shriveled and tough. In such a case the fruit cannot absorb syrup fast enough to replace the juice it loses. This is directly due to the thickness of the syrup and may take place regardless of rate of cooking.

Firm fruits will harden if cooked in a heavy sugar syrup. Therefore, they are started to cook in a thin syrup or in water. Extremely soft fruits, such as berries, on the other hand, are started in a fairly heavy syrup since their juice dilutes it almost at once, preventing shrinkage.

In the finished product the fruit should be clear, tender and juicy looking, the syrup thick and clear.

One fine, old-fashioned trick from the days when the housewife's preserves were the criterion of her ability as a cook is to use the juice of one fruit to make the syrup for preserving another. Very pretty color effects can be gained this way as well as wider variation of flavors. Red currant, black currant and apple juice were particularly favored. They may be substituted for water in the following recipes. Mixtures of fruits also make attractive and delicious preserves.

CANNING

Apricot Preserves

5 cups halved, peeled, hard-ripe apricots
(about 2 pounds)
4 cups sugar
¼ cup lemon juice

Thoroughly mix fruit with sugar and lemon juice. Cover tightly; let stand 4 to 5 hours in a cool place. Heat slowly to boiling, stirring occasionally until sugar dissolves. Cook rapidly until fruit is clear, about 30 minutes. As mixture thickens, stir frequently to prevent sticking. Pour, boiling hot, into hot jars. Adjust caps. Process 10-15 minutes in boiling water bath at simmering temperature (180-185°) Yield: about 4 half-pints.

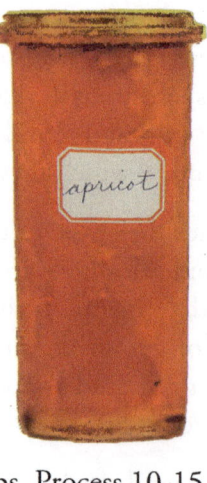

Cherry Preserves

2 pounds pitted tart red cherries
4 cups sugar

Drain juice from cherries. Add sugar to juice (if not enough juice to dissolve sugar, add a little water) and cook until sugar dissolves, stirring occasionally. Cool. Add cherries and cook rapidly until cherries become glossy, about 15 minutes. Cover and let stand 12 to 18 hours in a cool place. Bring to boiling and cook rapidly 1 minute. Pour, boiling hot into hot jars. Adjust caps. Process 10-15 minutes in boiling water bath at simmering temperature (180-185°) Yield: about 4 half-pints.

PRESERVES

Strawberry - Champagne Preserves

4 cups prepared fruit
(about 1 qt. fully ripe strawberries)
4 1/2 cups (2 lb.) sugar
1/4 cup sparkling white wine
Pectin as per product instructions
1/2 cup water

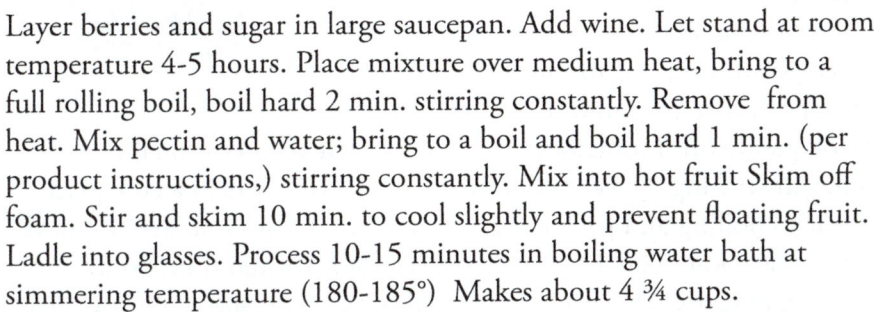

Layer berries and sugar in large saucepan. Add wine. Let stand at room temperature 4-5 hours. Place mixture over medium heat, bring to a full rolling boil, boil hard 2 min. stirring constantly. Remove from heat. Mix pectin and water; bring to a boil and boil hard 1 min. (per product instructions,) stirring constantly. Mix into hot fruit Skim off foam. Stir and skim 10 min. to cool slightly and prevent floating fruit. Ladle into glasses. Process 10-15 minutes in boiling water bath at simmering temperature (180-185°) Makes about 4 ¾ cups.

Pear Preserves

3 cups sugar
3 cups water
1 lemon, thinly sliced
6 medium cored, pared, hard-ripe pears, cut in quarters (about 2 lbs. before preparing)

Combine 1 ½ cups sugar and water; cook rapidly 2 minutes. Add pears and boil gently for 15 minutes. Add remaining sugar and lemon, stirring until sugar dissolves. Cook rapidly until fruit is clear, about 25 minutes. Cover and let stand 12 to 24 hours in a cool place. Pack fruit into hot jars, leaving ¼ inch head space. Cook sirup 3 to 5 minutes, or longer if too thin. Pour, boiling hot over fruit, leaving ¼-inch head space. Adjust caps. Process 20 minutes at 180 -185°F. in hot-water bath. Yield: about 5 half pints.

CANNING

Tomato Preserves

1 tablespoon mixed pickling spices
1 piece ginger root
4 cups sugar
2 lemons, thinly sliced
¾ cup water
1 ½ quarts small, firm, yellow, green or red peeled tomatoes (about 2 pounds)

Do not core tomatoes. Tie spices in a cheesecloth bag; add to sugar, lemon and water Simmer 15 minutes. Add tomatoes, cook gently until tomatoes become clear, stirring occasionally to prevent sticking. Cover and let stand 12 to 18 hours in a cool place. Heat to boiling and pack tomatoes and lemon into hot jars. Remove spice bag. Boil sirup 2 to 3 minutes, or longer if too thin; pour, boiling hot, over tomatoes leaving 1/4-inch head space. Adjust caps. Process half-pints and pints 20 minutes at 180 - 185° in hot-water bath. Yield: about 6 half-pints.

Strawberry Preserves

1 quart stemmed, firm, red ripe strawberries-
5 cups sugar
½ cup lemon juice

Berries with hollow cores should not be used. Combine berries and sugar; let stand 3 to 4 hours. Bring slowly to boiling, stirring occasionally until sugar dissolves. Cook rapidly until thick, about 20 minutes. Add lemon juice and continue cooking 10 minutes longer. Pour, boiling hot, into hot jars. Adjust caps. Process 15 minutes at 180 - 185° in hot-water bath. Yield: about 4 half-pints.

Peach Preserves

3 ½ cups sugar
2 cups water
5 cups sliced, peeled, hard-ripe peaches
(about 5 large)

Combine sugar and water and cook until sugar dissolves. Add peaches and cook rapidly until fruit becomes clear, stirring occasionally. Cover and let stand 12 to 18 hours in a cool place. Drain fruit and pack into hot jars, leaving 1/4-inch head space. Cook sirup rapidly 2 to 3 minutes, or longer if too thin. Pour over fruit, leaving 1/4-inch head space. Adjust caps. Process half-pints and pints 20 minutes at 180 - 185° in hot-water bath. Yield: about 6 half-pints.

Plum Preserves

5 cups pitted, tart plums
(about 2 ½ pounds)
4 cups sugar
1 cup water

Combine all ingredients. Bring slowly to boiling, stirring until sugar dissolves. Cook rapidly almost to jellying point, about 15 minutes, stirring frequently to prevent sticking Pour boiling hot into hot jars. Adjust caps. Process 15 minutes at 180 - 185° in hot-water bath. Yield: about 5 half-pints.

CONSERVES

Conserves are jam-like products made by cooking two or more fruits with sugar until the mixture will either round up in a spoon, like jam, or else flake from it as in the jelly test.

A true conserve contains nuts and raisins, but they may be added to, or omitted from, any recipe. Conserves should be made in small batches: cooked rapidly after sugar has dissolved; and nuts, if used, should be added the last 5 minutes of cooking time.

CANNING

Plum Conserves

2 1/2 quarts chopped, pitted plums
(about 4 pounds)
2 cups seedless raisins
6 cups sugar
2 cups broken pecans or other nuts
3/4 cup thinly sliced orange peel
1 ¾ cups chopped orange pulp (about 2 large)

Combine plums, orange pulp and peel, raisins and sugar; slowly bring to boiling, stirring occasionally until sugar dissolves. Cook rapidly almost to jellying point, about 15 to 20 minutes. As mixture thickens, stir frequently to prevent sticking. Add nuts the last 5 minutes of cooking. Pour, boiling hot, into hot jars. Adjust caps. Process 10-15 minutes at 180°-185° in hot-water bath. Yield: about 10 half-pints.

Blueberry Conserves

2 cups water
4 cups sugar
1/2 lemon, thinly sliced
1/2 orange, thinly sliced
1/2 cup seedless raisins
1 quart stemmed blueberries

Bring water and sugar to boiling Add lemon, orange and raisins; simmer 5 minutes. Add blueberries and cook rapidly until thick, about 30 minutes. As mixture thickens, stir frequently to prevent sticking Pour, boiling hot, into hot Ball jars. Adjust caps. Process 10-15 minutes at 180°-185° in hot-water bath. Yield about 4 half-pints.

CONSERVES

Dried Fruit Conserves

1 ½ cups cut-up dried apricots
1 ⅓ cups cut-up dried peaches
1 medium un-peeled orange, chopped
1 ⅓ cut-up dried pears - 3 cups water
2 cups sugar - 1 tablespoon lemon juice
½ cup seedless raisins - ½ teaspoon ground
cinnamon - ⅛ teaspoon ground cloves
½ cup chopped walnuts or other nuts.

Combine first 5 ingredients; cover and cook until fruits are tender, about 15 to 20 minutes. Uncover and add remaining ingredients except nuts. Slowly bring to boiling, stirring occasionally until sugar dissolves. Cook rapidly, stirring often, until thick, about 15 minutes. Add nuts the last 5 minutes of cooking. Pour, boiling hot, into hot jars. Adjust caps. Process 10-15 minutes at 180-185° in hot-water bath. Yield: about 5 half-pints.

Cherry Raspberry Conserve

3 cups raspberry pulp
4 cups sugar
3 cups pitted sweet cherries

To prepare raspberry pulp press berries through a sieve or food mill to remove seeds. Simmer cherries until tender add berry pulp and sugar. Cook slowly until sugar dissolves, stirring occasionally. Cook rapidly until thick, about 30 to 40 minutes. As mixture thickens, stir frequently to prevent sticking. Pour, boiling hot into hot jars. Adjust caps. Process 10-15 minutes at 180°-185° in hot-water bath. Yield: about 4 half-pints.

CANNING

Rhubarb-Strawberry-Orange Conserves

2 cups ½ inch slices rhubarb
1 cup seedless raisins
3 cups sugar
1 quart sliced strawberries
1 tablespoon grated orange peel
2 medium oranges, sectioned
¼ cup chopped walnuts & 1 cup seedless raisins

Combine rhubarb, raisins, orange peel and sections with sugar. Let stand several hours or overnight in a cool place. Add strawberries and bring slowly to boiling, stirring occasionally until sugar dissolves Cook rapidly until thick, about 25 minutes As mixture thickens, stir frequently to prevent sticking. Add nuts the last 5 minutes of cooking. Pour, boiling hot, into hot jars Adjust caps. Process 10-15 minutes at 180°-185° in hot-water bath. Yield: about 8 half-pints.

Peach Conserve

1 unpeeled orange chopped
5 cups sugar
7 cups chopped, peeled, firm-ripe peaches
(about 10 to 12 large)
1/2 teaspoon ground ginger
1/2 cup blanched, slivered almonds

Add orange to peaches; cook gently about 15 to 20 minutes. Add sugar and ginger Bring slowly to boiling, stirring occasionally until sugar dissolves. Cook rapidly until thick, about 15 minutes. As mixture thickens, stir occasionally to prevent sticking. Add nuts the last 5 minutes of cooking. Pour, boiling hot, into hot jars. Adjust caps. Process 10-15 minutes at 180°-185° in hot-water bath. Yield about 8 half-pints.

CONSERVES

Apple Blueberry Conserves

1 quart chopped, cored, pared tart apples (about 4 medium)
1 quart stemmed blueberries
6 cups sugar
½ cup seedless raisins
¼ cup lemon juice

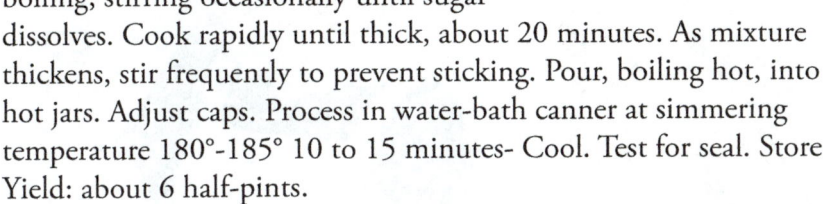

Combine all ingredients: slowly bring to boiling, stirring occasionally until sugar dissolves. Cook rapidly until thick, about 20 minutes. As mixture thickens, stir frequently to prevent sticking. Pour, boiling hot, into hot jars. Adjust caps. Process in water-bath canner at simmering temperature 180°-185° 10 to 15 minutes- Cool. Test for seal. Store. Yield: about 6 half-pints.

Grape Conserves

2 quarts stemmed grapes (about 4 lbs.)
6 cups sugar
1 cup chopped walnuts

Separate pulp from skins of grapes. Cook skins 15-20 minutes, adding ½ cup water to prevent sticking. Cook pulp without water until soft. Press through a sieve to remove seeds. Combine skins pulp and sugar. Bring slowly to boiling stirring until sugar dissolves. Cook rapidly until thick about 15 minutes. Stir frequently to prevent sticking. Add nuts last five minutes of cooking. Pour into hot jars. Adjust caps. Process 10 minutes at simmering 180°-185° in water-bath. Yield about 7 half-pints.

BUTTERS

Butters are made by cooking fruit pulp with sugar to a thick consistency which will spread easily. Spices may be added; the amount and variety depends upon personal taste. After sugar is added, butters should be cooked slowly and stirred frequently to prevent sticking. Less sugar is used in butters so it is advisable to process them at least 10 min. in a water-bath canner. If a fine-textured butter is desired, straining the pulp through a food mill and then re-straining through a fine-meshed sieve will make the job easier.

Fruit Butters are made from the pulp of fleshy fruit by boiling down the strained pulp and cooking with sugar and spices until thick and smooth. Less sugar in proportion to fruit is used in butters than in preserves or jams (usually ½ to ⅔ cup sugar to 1 cup fruit pulp). The pulp from the jelly bag can often be used for butters. Spices may be whole or ground. The latter tends to darken the mixture. If whole, they should be tied in a small bag and removed before pouring into the jars.

The usual procedure is as follows:
1. Prepare fruit.
2. Cook slowly in indicated amount of water until tender.
3. Rub through a sieve.
4. Continue cooking until it rounds on a spoon.
5. Measure.
6. Add indicated sugar and spices.
7. Cook rapidly, stirring constantly, until it "sheets" (page 5-6.)
8. Pour into clean, hot jars.

CANNING

Apricot Butter

1 1/2 quarts apricot pulp
3 cups sugar
2 tablespoons lemon juice

To prepare pulp cook pitted apricot halves until soft, adding only enough water to prevent sticking. Press through a sieve or food mill. Measure pulp. Add sugar; cook until thick, about 30 minutes. As mixture thickens,stir frequently to prevent sticking. Add lemon juice; pour hot into hot jars, leaving ¼ inch head space. Affix caps. Process pints and quarts about 10 minutes in boiling water bath at simmering temperature (180-185°) Yields: about 3 pints.

Pear Butter

2 quarts pulp
(about 20 medium fully ripe pears)
4 cups sugar
1 teaspoon grated orange rind
⅓ cup orange juice
½ teaspoon ground nutmeg

To prepare pulp quarter and core pears. Cook until soft, adding only enough water to prevent sticking. Press through a sieve or food mill. Measure pulp. Add remaining ingredients; cook until thick, about 15 minutes. As mixture thickens, stir frequently to prevent sticking. Pour hot into hot jars, leaving ¼ inch head space. Affix caps. Process pints and quarts about 10 minutes in boiling water bath at simmering temperature (180-185°) **Yields:** about 2 pints.

BUTTERS

Peach Butter

2 quarts peach pulp
(about 1 1/2 dozen medium, fully ripe peaches)
4 cups sugar

To prepare pulp, wash, scald, pit, peel and chop peaches; cook until soft, adding only enough water to prevent sticking. Press through a sieve or food mill. Measure pulp. Add sugar; cook until thick, about 30 minutes. As mixture thickens, stir frequently to prevent sticking. Pour, hot, into hot jars, leaving ¼ inch head space. Adjust caps. Process pints and quarts 10 minutes in boiling-water bath at simmering temperature (180 -185°) Yield: about 4 pints.

Apple Butter

2 dozen medium apples, quartered
(about 6 pounds)
3 cups sugar
1 ½ teaspoons ground cinnamon
2 quarts sweet cider
½ teaspoon ground cloves

Cook apples in cider until tender. Press through a sieve or food mill; measure 3 quarts apple pulp. Cook pulp until thick enough to round up in a spoon. As pulp thickens, stir frequently to prevent sticking. Add sugar and spices. Cook slowly, stirring frequently, until thick, about 1 hour. pour hot, into hot jars, leaving ¼ inch head space. Adjust caps. Process pints and quarts 10 minutes in boiling-water bath at simmering temperature (180 -185°) Yield: about 5 pints.

CANNING

Grape Butter

Wash, stem and stew ripe grapes with just enough water to cover bottom of pot until seeds are free. Press through colander. To each cup of pulp add half as much of sugar and continue cooking until thick. Continue cooking until it rounds on a spoon. Pour into clean, hot jars. Process 10 minutes in boiling-water bath at simmering temperature (180 -185°)

Plum Butter

Prick and cook with enough water to prevent burning until soft. Strain, measure, add 1 cup sugar to 2 cups pulp and boil until thick. Cook rapidly, stirring constantly, until it "sheets" (see Jelly Making). Pour into clean, hot jars. Process 10 minutes in boiling-water bath at simmering temperature (180 -185°)

Banana Butter

3 level cups crushed ripe bananas
7 level cups (3 lbs.) sugar
Juice of 1 lemon
Pectin as per product instructions

Crush bananas with masher to fine pulp and measure crushed fruit into large kettle. Add sugar and lemon juice, mix well and bring to a boil. Add pectin stirring constantly and bring again to a full boil and boil for 1 minute (per product instructions.) Stir constantly over entire bottom of kettle to prevent sticking. Remove from fire, and stir frequently for 8 minutes to cool slightly, which prevents fruit floating. Then pour quickly. Process 10 minutes in boiling-water bath at simmering temperature (180 -185°)

Tomato Butter

Peel 9 pounds tomatoes, cook until soft in 1 pint vinegar,. Strain and add 3 pounds sugar, 1 teaspoon ground mace, 2 teaspoons cinnamon, 1 teaspoon cloves and 1 teaspoon allspice. Boil until thick. Continue cooking until it rounds on a spoon. Pour into clean, hot jars. Process 10 minutes in boiling-water bath at simmering temperature (180 -185°)

MARMALADE

All the things that apply to jams apply to marmalades.
They are more likely to be made of large, solid fruits, particularly citrus. They can be distinguished from jams only by the larger and more important pieces of fruit that appear in them and by the definitely jelly-like consistency. They are made without water when possible for the same reason as jams and jellies. They are as easy to make and as useful as jams.

Briefly, marmalade making consists of softening the fruit, adding proportionate amounts of sugar, heating until thick and clear and pouring into sterile containers. The juices of marmalades will often "sheet" (see page 5-6) when they are done.

Fruits low in pectin are helped by the addition of apples or currants.

Like jams, marmalades must be closely watched while cooking lest they burn. Peels of citrus fruits do not cook soft in sugar syrups. Therefore, they are cooked tender in water first, then put into the syrup.

CANNING

Apricot - Pineapple Marmalade

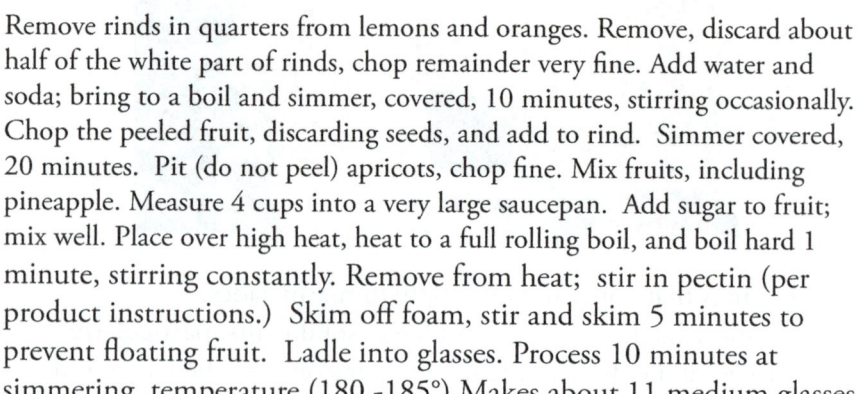

4 cups prepared seeded fruit (2 lemons, 2 oranges,
1 cup water, ⅛ teaspoon baking soda, ¾ lb. fully ripe
apricots, and one 8 ½ oz.. can crushed pineapple)
7 cups (3 lb.) sugar
Pectin as per product instructions

Remove rinds in quarters from lemons and oranges. Remove, discard about half of the white part of rinds, chop remainder very fine. Add water and soda; bring to a boil and simmer, covered, 10 minutes, stirring occasionally. Chop the peeled fruit, discarding seeds, and add to rind. Simmer covered, 20 minutes. Pit (do not peel) apricots, chop fine. Mix fruits, including pineapple. Measure 4 cups into a very large saucepan. Add sugar to fruit; mix well. Place over high heat, heat to a full rolling boil, and boil hard 1 minute, stirring constantly. Remove from heat; stir in pectin (per product instructions.) Skim off foam, stir and skim 5 minutes to prevent floating fruit. Ladle into glasses. Process 10 minutes at simmering temperature (180 -185°) Makes about 11 medium glasses.

Kumquat Marmalade

3 quarts water
1 ½ cups chopped seeded orange pulp
(about 2 medium)
2 cups thinly sliced kumquats (about 2 dozen)
⅓ cup lemon juice
1 ½ cups sliced orange peel (about 2 medium)
Sugar, about 9 cups

Add water to fruit; cover and let stand in a cool place overnight. Bring to boiling and cook until peel is tender. To each cup of fruit mixture, add 1 cup sugar. Stir until sugar is dissolved. Cook rapidly to jellying point, about 45 minutes. Stir occasionally to prevent sticking. Pour, boiling hot, int hot jars. Adjust caps. Process 10 minutes at simmering temperature (180 -185°) Yield: about 8 half-pints.

MARMALADE

Grapefruit Marmalade

⅔ cup thinly sliced grapefruit
1 ½ cups chopped seeded grapefruit pulp (about 1)
1 quart water
Sugar, about 4 cups

Cover grapefruit peel with water; boil 10 minutes and drain. Repeat 2 or 3 times. To drained peel, add chopped pulp and 1 quart water Cover and let stand 12 to 18 hours in a cool place. Cook rapidly until peel is tender, about 40 minutes. Measure fruit and liquid Add 1 cup sugar for each cup of fruit mixture. Bring slowly to boiling, stirring until sugar dissolves. Cook rapidly almost to jellying point, about 30 to 35 minutes Stir occasionally to prevent sticking Pour, boiling hot. into hot jars. Adjust caps. Process 10 minutes at simmering temperature (180 -185°) Yields about 3 half-pints

Carrot - Orange Marmalade

4 cups grated raw carrots
4 lemons
2 oranges
Sugar
Water, about 6 cups

Squeeze oranges and lemons, save the juice. Grate the rinds of 1 orange and 2 lemons and cook until tender, about 30 minutes in 3 cups of water. Add the grated carrots and 3 cups of water and cook until tender-about 20 minutes. Add the orange and lemon juice. Measure the mixture. For each cup of this mixture add ⅔ cup sugar. Boil to the marmalade stage, about an hour Add pinch salt. Pour hot marmalade into hot jars and seal. Process 10 minutes at simmering temperature (180 -185°) Yield: about 10-11 half-pints.

CANNING

Orange Marmalade

1 quart orange peel, thinly sliced (about 6 large)
1 quart seeded orange pulp (about 6 large)
1 cup thinly sliced lemon (about 2 large)
Sugar, about 6 cups
⅓ cup lemon juice
1 ½ quarts water

Add water to fruit and simmer 5 minutes Cover and let stand 12 to 18 hours in a cool place. Cook rapidly until peel is tender, about 1 hour. Measure fruit and liquid, add 1 cup sugar for each cup of fruit. Bring slowly to boiling, stirring until sugar dissolves. Cook rapidly to jellying point, about 25 minutes. As mixture thickens, stir occasionally to prevent sticking. Pour, boiling hot, into hot jars. Adjust caps. Process 10 minutes . Yield: about 7 half-pints

Cherry Marmalade

1 orange with peel, seeded, finely chopped
4 cups pitted sweet cherries
3 ½ cups sugar
¼ cup lemon juice

Cover chopped orange with water and boil until soft; cool. Add cherries, lemon juice and sugar to orange. Bring slowly to boiling stirring until sugar is dissolved Cook rapidly to jellying point, about 35 minutes, stirring frequently. Pour, boiling hot, into hot jars. Adjust caps. Process 10 to 15 minutes at simmering temperature (180 -185°) Yield: about 4 half-pints.
Note: If sour cherries are to be used, reduce lemon juice to 2 tablespoons.

Peach - Orange Marmalade

2 quarts chopped, peeled, firm-ripe peaches (about 10 large)
1 ½ cups chopped seeded orange pulp (about 2 medium)
¾ cup sliced orange peel
2 tablespoons lemon juice
5 cups sugar

Combine all ingredients; bring slowly to boiling, stirring occasionally until sugar dissolves. Cook rapidly until thick, about 20 minutes. As mixture thickens, stir frequently to prevent sticking. Pour, boiling hot. into hot jars. Adjust caps. Process 10-15 minutes at simmering temperature. (180 -185°) Yield: about 8 half-pints

Quince - Apple Marmalade

3 cups chopped, cored, pared quinces (about 6 medium)
2 cups chopped, cored, pared tart apples (about 3 medium)
Sugar, about 2 ½ cups

When preparing quinces, discard all gritty parts. Add water to quinces just to cover, cook rapidly until tender Add apples and cook 10 minutes. Measure fruit and liquid. Add ¾ cup sugar to each cup fruit mixture. Bring slowly to boiling, stirring until sugar dissolves. Cook rapidly almost to boiling point, about 15 to 20 minutes, stir frequently to prevent sticking. Pour, boiling hot. into hot jars. Adjust caps Process 15 minutes at simmering temperature. (180 -185°) Yield: about 4 half-pints.

CPSIA information can be obtained at www.ICGtesting.com
Printed in the USA
LVOW01s1716240713

344440LV00015B/26/P